August 12, 2000

For my precious daughter,
Elizabeth, and her precious
daughter, Morgan.

Love,

Mom and Grandma

**Other giftbooks by Helen Exley:**

Mothers...                    To My Lovely Mother
Womens Thoughts...      To A Very Special Daughter
The Love Between Fathers and Daughters

Published simultaneously in 1995 by Exley Publications in Great
Britain, and Exley Giftbooks in the USA.

12

Edited and pictures selected by Helen Exley.
The moral right of the author has been asserted.
Pictures researched by Image Select International.
Typesetting by Delta, Watford.
Printed in China.

**Exley Publications Ltd, 16 Chalk Hill, Watford, Herts
WDl 4BN, United Kingdom.
Exley Publications LLC, 232 Madison Avenue, Suite 1206,
New York, NY 10016, USA.**

# THE LOVE BETWEEN
# *Mothers and Daughters*

*A Helen Exley Giftbook*

**EXLEY**
NEW YORK • WATFORD, UK

"…the daughter never ever gives up on the mother, just as the mother never gives up on the daughter. There is a tie here so strong that nothing can break it. I called it 'the unbreakable bond'."

RACHEL BILLINGTON, b.1942,
FROM THE "SUNDAY TIMES",
MARCH 13, 1994

*"She tried in every way to understand me, and she succeeded. It was this deep, loving understanding as long as she lived that more than anything else helped and sustained me on my way to success."*

MAE WEST (1892-1980)

"She [my mother] is the one person who looks into my heart, sees its needs, and tries to satisfy them. She is also always trying to make me be what she thinks it is best for me to be. She tells me how to do my hair, what clothes I shoud wear. She wants to love and control at the same time. Her love is sustained and deep. Sometimes I feel like a drowning person, saved by the pulling and tugging, saved by the breath of air that is her caring."

BELL HOOKS,
FROM "DOUBLE STITCH"

*"A loving and careful mother both recognises and even protects her daughter's autonomy and also helps her dance out confidently on to a wider stage."*

**RACHEL BILLINGTON, b.1942,**
**FROM "THE GREAT UMBILICAL"**

*"My mother raised me, and then freed me."*

**MAYA ANGELOU, b.1928**

"There is nothing on earth like the moment of seeing one's first baby. Men scale other heights, but there is no height like this simple one, occurring continuously throughout all the ages in musty bedrooms, in palaces, in caves and desert places. I looked at this rolled-up bundle … and knew again I had not created her. She was herself apart from me. She had her own life to lead, her own destiny to accomplish; she just came past me to this earth. My job was to get her to adulthood and then push her off."

KATHARINE TREVELYAN, FROM "THROUGH MINE OWN EYES"

*"Then someone placed her in my arms. She looked up at me. The crying stopped. Her eyes melted through me, forging a connection in me with their soft heat."*

SHIRLEY MACLAINE, b.1934

"Gradually I began to realise that she liked me, that she had no option to liking me, and that unless I took great pains to alienate her she would go on liking me, for a couple of years at least. It was very pleasant to receive such uncritical love, because it left me free to bestow love; my kisses were met by small warm rubbery unrejecting cheeks and soft dovey mumblings of delight."

MARGARET DRABBLE, b.1939,
FROM "THE MILLSTONE"

*I wonder if you remember how
we loved long days in the country?
How you laughed when we swung
you in the air? How we all put on
our bright gloves and went crunching
into the snow? Your little red bobble
hat? Your tiny boots?
I remember. I always will.*

HELEN THOMSON, b.1943

"I have so much I can teach her and pull out of her. I would say you might encounter defeats but you must never be defeated. I would teach her to love a lot. Laugh a lot at the silliest things and be very serious. I would teach her to love life, I could do that."

MAYA ANGELOU, b.1928

"The baby is born and your life is changed more than you ever dreamed. You find you have sprouted invisible antennae that pick up every alteration in breathing, every variation in temperature, every nuance of expression in your tiny daughter. No-one tells you that the change is irreversible. That you will feel in your heart every pain, every loss, every disappointment, every rebuff, every cruelty that she experiences life long."

**PAM BROWN, B.1928**

"She is very touching in her sweet little marks of affection. Once or twice, when I have seemed unhappy about little things, she has come and held up her sweet mouth to be kissed. Last night I was in pain, and made a sort of moan. She was lying by me, apparently asleep; but as if her gentle instinct of love prompted her even then, she pressed to me, saying, 'Kiss, Mama.' These are trifles, but how very precious may the remembrance of them become…"

ELIZABETH GASKELL (1810-1865),
FROM "MY DIARY"

"Your first swan. Your first day by the sea. Your first walk through a field of spring flowers. The first time you heard and loved Chopin. In sharing your childhood discoveries, I have relived my own."

MARION C. GARRETTY, b.1917

## Hush – Oh Hush!

*Hush – Oh hush! my little wild one,*
*Hear the stirring in the hollow,*
*With thy restless little crying*
*Thou wilt wake the small*
*sea-swallow.*
*Dearer than the bread of raupo,*
*Dearer than the sweet konini,*
*Dearer than the dead to Tane,*
*Yea, so dear art thou until me.*
*Sleep, my wild karaka berry,*
*Sleep, my red-lipped rata-blossom,*
*Ate! Ate! Ate! Ate!*

EILEEN DUGGAN (MAORILAND)

"No relationship is as highly charged as that between mother and daughter, or as riddled with expectations that could, like a landmine, detonate with a single misstep, a solitary stray word that, without warning, wounds or enrages. And no relationship is as bursting with possibilities of goodwill and understanding."

**VICTORIA SECUNDA,**
**FROM "WHEN YOU AND YOUR MOTHER**
**CAN'T BE FRIENDS"**

"My love for her and my hate for her are so bafflingly intertwined that I can hardly see her. I never know who is who. She is me and I am she and we're all together."

**ERICA JONG, b.1942**

"The daughter tends to resent her mother as most people resent the imposers of rules, but even more so because there are more rules for daughters than for sons."

**PAULA CAPLAN**

"If ever I raise my eyebrows at your dress, dear, remind me of winkle-picker stilettos, The Sack, near-white lipstick and the Doe-Eyed look. As I reminded my mother of hobble skirts and cloche hats. And she reminded her mother that she stuffed her bosom with old socks. And she reminded…."

PAM BROWN, b.1928

"My mother won't admit it, but I've always been a disappointment to her. Deep down inside, she'll never forgive herself for giving birth to a daughter who refuses to launder aluminum foil and use it over again."

ERMA BOMBECK, b.1927

<u>Precepts for the guidance
of a daughter.</u>
Remember Evelyn was not the first
Norman King of England.
Wash your hands.
When you have washed them,
hold a book in them.
Diminish your calves.
Pluck your arms.
Get up early, but not too early.
Don't gobble it; it turns maidens
and turkey-cocks purple.
Don't swear.
Assume the power of reading,
if you have it not.

ELIZABETH GASKELL (1810-1865)

*"Within minutes, we're peddling away, the two of us, a genetic sewing machine that runs on limitless love. It's my belief that between mothers and daughters there is a kind of blood-hyphen that is, finally, indissoluble."*

CAROL SHIELDS,
FROM "SWANN"

"What do we mean by the nurture of daughters? What is it we wish we had, or could have, as daughters; could give, as mothers? Deeply and primally we need trust and tenderness; surely this will always be true of every human being, but women growing into a world so hostile to us need a very profound kind of loving in order to learn to love ourselves."

ADRIENNE RICH, b.1939

*"My Dear Mary,*

*How lonely the house seems – I never knew before how well you helped to fill it. I am anxious to hear of your first impressions of the city and how you like your new home. Every since you went away, I have been wondering if it was as hard for you to go out into the world as it was for me to have you go.*

*Don't write short, hurried letters, simply stating facts in their tersest form, but tell me all your thoughts and dreams and plans, your worries and trials, and we will talk them over as two comrades.... If there is anything in my life that can be of value to you, I want you to have it; if I can save you a stumble or a single false step, I want to do it, but the only way I can do it is to know your heart.*

*Your loving mother."*

**FLORENCE WENDEROTH SAUNDERS,
FROM "LETTERS TO A BUSINESS GIRL", 1908**

"For I realised that the process of mothering, as described in a man's world, supposed children at an age to be 'mothered' in the home. But the reality of mothering goes on throughout the entire life of the mother. A bad mother might make a good grandmother. Once a mother, always a mother – even if your daughter is seventy. The relationship changes, of course, but is no less important."

RACHEL BILLINGTON, b.1942,
FROM THE "SUNDAY TIMES", MARCH 13, 1994

*A daughter and her mother*

*are never free of one*

*another –*

*no matter how they*

*disagree.*

*For they are so entwined*

*in heart and mind*

*that, gladly or unwillingly,*

*they share each love, each*

*joy, each sorrow and each*

*bitter wrong*

*life-long.*

**PAM BROWN, b.1928**

"My mother taught me to walk proud and tall 'as if the world was mine.'"
**SOPHIA LOREN, b.1934**

"My mother's best advice to me was: 'Whatever you decide to do in life, be sure that the joy of doing it does not depend upon the applause of others, because in the long run we are, all of us, alone.'"
**ALI MACGRAW**

"Whatever beauty or poetry is to be found in my little book is owing to your interest in and encouragement of all my efforts from the first to the last; and if ever I do anything to be proud of, my greatest happiness will be that I can thank you for that, as I may do for all the good there is in me; and I shall be content to write if it gives you pleasure."
**LOUISA MAY ALCOTT (1832-1888), TO HER MOTHER**

"My mother has stopped talking. She raises her eyebrows, asking me to respond to her. Soon I know if I hold silence she will take a deep breath and straighten her shoulders. 'Daughter,' she will say, in a voice that is stern and admonishing, 'always a woman must be stronger than the most terrible circumstance. You know what my mother used to say? Through us, the women of the world, only through us can everything survive.' An image comes to me. I see generations of women bearing a flame. It is hidden, buried deep within, yet they are handing it down from one to another, burning. It is a gift of fire, transported from a world far off and far away, but never extinguished. And now, in this very moment, my mother imparts the care of it to me. I must keep it alive, I must manage not to be consumed by it, I must hand it on when the time comes to my daughter."

**KIM CHERNIN,
FROM "IN MY MOTHER'S HOUSE"**

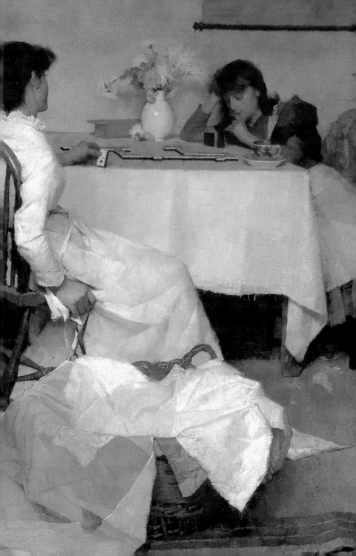

"The relationship between modern daughters – especially grown-up daughters – and their mothers never ceases to fascinate me. It is warm and close, and loving. It is also frank and terse, and ruthless. It ranges over every conceivable topic, from their utmost dreams to their inmost dreads, and from the strength of their sauces to the colour of their handbags. Mothers and daughters, in my experience, no longer have secrets from each other worth talking about. All is grist to the never-ending mill."

**GODFREY SMITH**

"…women pass on from mother to daughter a heredity far more real than anything shown on the traditionally male genealogical table. Every woman feels it when she looks back at her mother or forward to her daughter. It expresses itself at an everyday level of practical caring and at a deeper level of emotional self-identification and wholeness. But, above all, it is a teacher of love – the first teacher and the most important, from which all other love stems."

RACHEL BILLINGTON, b..1942, FROM "THE GREAT UMBILICAL"

*extract from*
*POEM TO HER DAUGHTER*

*Daughter, take this amulet*
*tie it with cord and caring*
*I'll make you a chain of*
*coral and pearl*
*to glow on your neck.*
*I'll dress you nobly.*
*A gold clasp too – fine, without flaw*
*to keep with you always.*
*When you bathe, sprinkle perfume, and*
*weave your hair in braids.*
*String jasmine for the counterpane.*
*Wear your clothes like a bride,*
*for your feet anklets, bracelets for*
*your arms…*
*Don't forget rosewater,*
*don't forget henna for the palms of*
*your hands.*

**MWANA KUPONA MSHAM**

"I am an onlooker on my daughter's dance, which I ... made possible because she came through me ... I'm not part of her dance. Yet whenever she takes a pause and needs someone to talk to, I am there. But that special dance with the child and the future is hers."

LIV ULLMANN, b.1939

*"What I wanted most for my daughter was that she be able to soar confidently in her own sky, wherever that might be, and if there was space for me as well I would, indeed, have reaped what I had tried to sow."*

HELEN CLAES

**Acknowledgements:** The publishers are grateful for permission to reproduce copyright material. While every effort has been made to trace copyright holders, the publishers would be pleased to hear from any not here acknowledged.

Rachel Billington: extracts from "The Great Umbilical" published by Hutchinson/Random Century, 1994. Reprinted by permission of David Higham Associates Ltd; extracts also from the "Sunday Times" 13 March 1994; Kim Chernin: extract from "In My Mother's House"; Margaret Drabble: extract from "The Millstone" published by Weidenfeld and Nicolson; Eileen Duggan: extract from "Your Baby Girl" published by Piatkus Books; Godfrey Hodgson: extract from The Sunday Times; Bell Hooks: extract from "Reflections Of A 'Good' Daughter" taken from "Double Stitch" published by Harper Perennial, a division of HarperCollins, USA, 1991; Mwana Kupona Msham: extract "From Poem To Her Daughter"; Victoria Secunda: extract from "When You And Your Mum Can't Be Friends" published by Cedar, a division of Reed Consumer Books, 1993; Katherine Trevelyan: extract from "Through Mine Own Eyes".